INTO TEMPTATION

Sophia Blackwell was born in Newcastle and read English at Oxford, where she discovered Slam poetry. Since then she has performed with some of the biggest names in spoken word at a variety of venues including the South Bank Centre, Soho Theatre and Roundhouse in London and the O2 Academy Oxford, as well as several feature slots at Glastonbury, Wychwood, The Big Green Gathering, TruckFest and The Big Chill. She lives in North London.

INTO TEMPTATION

Sophia Blackwell

First published in 2009 by Tollington Press, Machynlleth, Wales, UK
Reprinted 2011, 2015
www.tollingtonpress.co.uk

www.sophiablackwell.co.uk

A catalogue record for this book is available from the British Library.

ISBN 978-0-9560173-1-4

Author photograph © Stephen McLaren
Cover design by Sarah Wood
Typeset by Helen Sandler

Printed and bound in Wales by Y Lolfa, Talybont, Ceredigion,
on FSC-certified paper

CONTENTS

1: MAD LOVE

2: NO ANGELS

3: ORDINARY JOYS

To Mum & Dad

Acknowledgements

With thanks, love and respect to the following:

Steve Larkin for getting me started and for constant inspiration and delight, Alan Buckley, George Roberts and Joe Butler for being the least po-faced Poetry Peer Group ever, and Roman Krznaric for finding me work that kept my mind and wallet full when no one else would. Massive thanks to Jen Roberts for her stellar example of glamorous wilderness living, helping me get established and introducing me to the best gigs and people in London, and to my best friends Ella Genty and Helen Higginbottom for their encouragement and support. Finally, thanks to my parents for teaching me to scream, dream and be happy.

'Hair', 'Knives' and 'Cover' first appeared in *The Nail* and excerpts from several poems appeared in *The Oxford Muse's Guide to an Unknown University*. Thanks also to Hammer and Tongue, the Catweazle Club and Behind the Mic, where these poems were performed for the first time and where I've met most of my favourite people.

Lead me not into temptation; I can find the way myself.
—*Rita Mae Brown*

1

MAD LOVE

The Monster in Me

I met you, a barefoot girl, not sure what this world might be.
You nestled in me, a pearl on the bed of a bitter sea.
Bursting with flowers and candles and shootout movie trysts
with crosses round my neck and holy water on my wrists,
clanking with rings and ankle-chains, I prayed that you wouldn't see
something about your untouched skin unleashed the monster in me,

And made me a hard-faced diva with a stretched, unblinking stare,
sodden with drink and downers, face a painted prayer.
Stiff as a thrift-shop icon, Our Lady trampling snakes,
a blank-eyed bloodied saint who holds her lopped-off breasts like cakes.
Offering you the platter, I threw in my heart for free.
Something about your unkissed lips unearthed the monster in me,

And made me a snarling creature, my muzzle flecked with meat,
ready to kill and nuzzle, to fight and mate and eat,
but not sure what I wanted – to be stroked by you, or feed.
Your pale surprise met my piss-gold eyes, narrow and hot with need.
Turning in wounded circles made me too tired to flee.
Something in your uneven smile unnerved the monster in me,

And made me a skull-collector, glinting in mirrored shades,
an armoured guard around me and a crucifix of blades
that could strip your skin down to chamois-thin, my bloody Valentine.
I'd have kept your heart in my ice compartment if that might make
     you mine.
But when you said, *No more of this, I want you, can't you see?*
Something in your uncertain kiss unarmed the monster in me,

And I left you, a barefoot girl, not sure what this world might be,
stripped of my claws and clutter, empty, alone and free.
Without the props and hunger, we didn't quite convince.
I couldn't stay a monster, and Lord knows I'm no prince –
I'm human. When push comes to shove, we're just not meant to be.
Our not-quite-unrequited love undid the monster in me.

Gifts

I do not need the priest, the flowers, the blessing.
I'd rather keep the nights we paint the town,
the Sundays that we slouch through without dressing.

Our aisles are all the streets we wander down.
Your style of church is Puritan John Knox,
I'm used to blood and gold. No virgin's gown,

no diamond in a plumply cushioned box –
my hands are naked, ready to receive you.
No *any-lawful-reason* paradox,

no scripted lines to tell you I believe you.
My body is an anarchist, a lout
that doesn't worship you – or want to leave you.

What worldly goods I own you know about.
I give you trailing Glastonbury flags,
the grey North Sea, my memories, the shout

of blues, and ripe tomatoes in striped bags,
and dingy dives with walls of straw-bound wine,
and jewel-box burlesque theatres off main drags.

You give me joy. You make my life a line
that works much better in your own translation.
This wild abundance when our worlds combine

is one big wedding feast, one long vacation,
the candles lit, and your contentment mine,
each hour a gift, each day a celebration.

Don't Tell Me the Truth about Love

Tell me it's *all around me*.
Tell me it's *all you need,*
That it lifts us up where we belong
like those slick old songs agreed.
It's the *greatest thing you'll ever learn,*
and it *don't cost a thing.*
Tell me that acid doesn't burn.
Tell me that I can sing.

Will I turn into one of those women
whose only known pronoun is *we,*
like 'Saturday, yeah – we went swimming,
then watched the whole *Lost* DVD...'?
That's my life, and I let it complete me,
while those tales often fail to compel me.
(Has that irony missed me completely?
I think that it has. But don't tell me).

Tell me that it might let me off
just 'cause it likes my face.
Tell me it doesn't need air, or light,
or room, or time, or space.
Tell me that it's the cold white wine
chilling in the fridge,
not a bottle of snake-oil cure-all,
not my piece of the Brooklyn Bridge.

Will we ever turn into those lovers
that we try to ignore in cafés,
who aren't sure what to do with each other
in the face of immeasurable days?

Could the nest that we spent so long making
Crack apart in the wind and expel me?
What if it's ripe for the taking?
I know it could be. But don't tell me.

Tell me it's hard as diamonds,
tell me we've earned this peace,
it's a crime we got away with,
it's a room without a lease,
it's a store of easy pleasures
and a source of quiet pride,
and these saved-up, grown-up treasures
don't look simple to divide.

Could I ever get over the freezing fear
of a time when I can't see or hear her,
when I feel like forgetting to breathe if I hear
of an accident anywhere near her?
Is it normal to feel this about her –
while I doubt I could ever forget her,
when I think of a future without her,
I wish I'd just plain never met her?

Who thought of love as the remedy
for whatever's ever hurt us?
Will this end with me drinking neat JD
watching films by Richard Curtis?
Will I howl in municipal places
like a junkie in need of a hit,
surrounded by miserable faces
and not really bothered by it?

Am I realist, deluded, asleep or awake?
Can I hide this, abide this, preserve this?
Is this too much to take? Is there too much at stake?
Is my table so full I deserve this?
Can I say we'll be happy together?
Will the things that I cling to repel me?
What's the closest you get to forever?
Who knows? You don't know. So don't tell me.

Cover

We stood beneath the cover of the night
and joked that we would never mate for life,
while all around us, sharp in black and white,
young girls in trousers played at man and wife.
Our words were brittle, breakable and bright.
They swarmed like smoke, a falling cloud above you.
I swore I'd do my best to keep things light,
commit myself to trying not to love you.

Our evenings were sloshed in gin and smoke,
hazy and dense – we never blew our covers.
Our friends clinked glasses, creasing at the joke –
the two sworn loners playing swooning lovers.
We drank, played cards and disappeared in song.
Nothing was broken, nothing lost or taken,
but when I held your glance a beat too long,
the whole sophisticated sham was shaken.

Then when they left we fell into each other,
laughing them off like a disjointed dream.
Beneath your foreign grandma's patchwork cover,
I mapped your bones, your veins, each buried stream
of blue beneath the cream. Your eyes screwed tight
and opened, letting in my face above you.
Watching you sleep in uninvited light,
I felt the pull of trying not to love you.

No one, including us, still got the joke.
It was a fling, we said, like any other,
with no more form or substance than the smoke
we blew the day that I shrugged on my cover

to watch you ending what had never been,
your eyes still bright, but breaking into streams
like fractured light, which I had never seen
or wanted to, except in smothered dreams.

Dreams where we said the words that we'd held tight,
where we were known, and breathed outside your door.
Now I walk quickly through the falling night,
loving the silence still, but craving more.
How can I heal the hurts I've seen you smother?
Why am I aching as I rise above you?
We've swapped one source of anguish for another.
My heart is breaking trying not to love you.

Goodnight Moon

Tell me a tale, you said,
'cause it ain't paint that taints your pale lips red.
They were coloured by your mother a month before your birth
when she cut her hand on an old tin can and she brought you to this earth
singing, 'Let her hair be raven, let her skin be white,
let her not go waving down the roadsides of the night.'
Your father let you grow till your blood began to flow,
then his new wife paid the hunter to drag you through the snow,
where the eyes your mother gave you made him melt and set you free.
She told him to bring back your heart, so leave your heart with me.

We were babes in the wood trapped by shadows of doubt.
We climbed into your wardrobe but couldn't get out
to the fantasy land that you told me about
where we'd be together and never without
each other, forever. The woods were so deep
but when I was scared, then you sang me to sleep.
Goodnight forest, goodnight sky,
Goodnight one more day gone by...
You were always out of tune.
Goodnight moon.

Spin me a yarn, you said.
Charm this straw to golden thread.
I sat spinning in my room until my fingers bled.
My back was racked, my fingers cracked and the straw was stained with red.
And now you're at my door, I'm no princess any more.
The longest that I watch my face is when I wash the floor.
And when I catch a glimpse of the mirror in the hall
your voice no longer tells me I'm the fairest of them all.

We were babes in the wood trapped by shadows of doubt.
I climbed into your closet to make you come out.
Now we live in that world that you told me about,
but we're older, and colder, and too scared to shout
and to chant and to dance like we knew that we could
when no one could hear us, alone in the wood.
Oh, baby girl, baby girl, fly away home.
Your house is on fire and those children are gone.
Rich girl, poor girl, beggar girl, thief,
Growing up is a kind of grief.
Coulda, shoulda, pudding and pie,
You kissed girls and it made me cry.
So no more playing in the trees,
no more praying on my knees,
wishing time away too soon.
Goodnight moon.

Sing me a song, you said,
'Cause it ain't wrong to paint those strong lips red
as berries in December, for that blood your mother shed
was to keep you safe, remember, from the demons in her head.
But now you've bowed your head, you're not singing like you should.
You lost me when you fled from the shadows of the wood.

Tell me a lie, I said. *See if your words can buy my bread.*
My mother's prayer was not about my skin or hair or eyes.
No, she cut her hand on an old tin can and said, 'Let my girl be wise.
Let my baby fight. Let my baby feel.
Let her sleep a thousand nights, but make her wake up real.'

We were babes in the wood trapped by shadows of doubt.
You climbed into my head and you never got out.
I can't even recall what those tales were about,
but I know there are things I can manage without.
So goodnight standing cold and numb,
waiting for the night to come,
morning, evening, afternoon.
Goodbye princess, hello grafter.
Hello life and hello laughter.
Hello, *all right ever after?*
Goodnight moon.

Born Again

There'd be no wars if we all woke this way.
All sticky, folded velvet curves, we purr
like half-blind cubs, and mewl and squint and say
Just five more minutes, staying where we were,
in limbo. Once you said, beneath a yawn,
A hazy sentence far from adulthood
from that vast poem – *I am not yet born.*
Protect you – girl, I only wish I could.
I steel myself to leave you every day
that stalks us, grey, unknowable and new.
I grow more layers as I walk away,
folding away the part of me that's you,
wishing that warmth between us both could stay,
wanting the day to hold you like I do.

Paris in the Spring

I closed our door behind me. She was there
to be his model, poised above my chair
like staying still would hurt. I couldn't bear
to hold her gaze, but she was everywhere.

That short black hair, not fair like him. I'd tried
to be her friend. I guess I knew he'd lied –
black hair, caught on my coat? Not satisfied,
but what's a girl to do? I had my pride.

Tea time. The married woman's alibi,
a darker sky, fur coats, a little lie.
We walked and smelled the rain, his Muse and I.
Our talk was small, and flickered like a sigh,

shook like the light outside our small hotel,
that peachy red. Our breathing rose and fell.
Take me, she laughed. To heaven or to hell,
I didn't know, myself. And she could tell.

I didn't know myself, and she could tell.
Take me. She laughed, *to heaven or to hell?*
That peachy red. Our breathing rose and fell,
shook like the light outside our small hotel.

Our talk was small, and flickered like a sigh.
We walked and smelled the rain, his Muse and I.
A darker sky. Fur coats. A little lie –
Tea time. The married woman's alibi,

but what's a girl to do? I had my pride,
black hair caught on my coat. Not satisfied
to be her friend, I guess. I knew he'd lied.
That short black hair. Not fair. Like him, I'd tried

to hold her gaze, but she was everywhere,
like staying still would hurt. I couldn't bear
to be his model, poised above my chair.
I closed our door behind me. She was there.

I Marry You Alone

Alone in an Italian restaurant
in a strange town, my arms bent round a book,
I act the business bitch, the bitter aunt,
the awkward girl. The waiters crane to look,
unsure of me. My phone purrs into life,
your name comes up – a scrap of something known
that draws me closer, feeling like your wife
as your words hold me, make this place my own.
I'm in the bath. It's dark. You know how much you
feel near to me? You're so close I could touch you.
I gulp my wine, push back my hair, and see
my hand stretch forward, bare of glint and stone,
just flesh and bone. My flesh and bone. It's me.
I'm touching you. I marry you alone.

I thought I'd need a house with many floors
to hold our breathing lives in separate walls.
We'd meet when ready, leave by different doors,
arrive by walkways, tiptoe in the halls,
but now I'm happy just to share a room,
this night we're in, my skin, your text, my phone,
a vast wet sky, my strangeness here, the gloom,
the screen that mists and holds the kiss you've blown,
this tiny x. I cup and hold your text.
The waiter's drawn a heart shape on my cheque.
This wild wide night's contraction and expansion
leaves me adrift beyond my comfort zone.
You were the one who dared to trash the mansion
of love I chose. I marry you alone.

The signs don't help me, every road redoubles.
I find my hotel down a random street,
and, like a dream, a stream of floating bubbles
flows round me from a nightclub door. We meet
in darkness here, as fragile as their kiss
against my skin. I like life on my own
but know that we can't love too long like this –
we can't protect ourselves, so why postpone?
You'll be with me when I turn out the light.
I'll be the pillow in your arms tonight.
Back in my room I ache to hear your voice
and yet I'm glad to get your answerphone.
I'm scared of what I'll say. I've made a choice.
I taste the night. I marry you alone.

This Is Not the Poem about You

This is not the poem about you.
Don't think I'm being super-mean or scrupulously cool,
but I want to tell you now that even when I'm ninety-two
and necking Tesco Value Gin while bombing down the street
on a nifty tartan scooter with my fags under the seat,
teaching classical translations with Sapphic implications
in an all-girl's boarding school,
this is something I still won't do.
I will never write the poem about you.
So don't cringe
at the prospect of some emotional binge
to impress the poetic lunatic fringe
I'm affiliated to.

This is not the poem that wins Slams.
This is not one of those gushy, syrup-slushy meditations
on iambic masturbation by those big I-Ams
that kind of makes you doubt their reproductive education:
Oh baby, you're so hot,
You're like Adonis and Beyoncé's daughter.
I could swallow every goddamn pair of pants you've got
Without one glass of water.
And I can't help thinking, isn't this a drag?
What are you supposed to do, wave your scorecard and go
'Oh my God, that person's had a shag! … Eight point two for trying.'
And I'm not denying, I would be lying if I said I wasn't the kind of person
to get smashed, occasionally flash and generally say any old trash
for one iota of some complete and utter stranger's attention. It's true.
But I have no intention of mentioning you.
Even for a nine point two.

And this is not the poem intended to define you.
Could you draw a line through an exploding star?
I'd rather use my tongue for things that wouldn't undermine you
'cause you shine, you make a million poems in the ways you choose
    to live,
and no scribbles on a page, no strutting on a stage
could make you any more than what you are.
I'd rather try to part the night that parts us two
like Canute and Cuchulain tried to fight the ocean,
but I would never dare to make a sad statue
of your far-flung-out da Vinci world in motion.

And this is not the poem that says I know you
because I know what you're about.
If I wanted to file you away, I'd just dial you
when feeling manic and messianic and a bit pissed –
or get a pen and paper, make a list.
Foods you like – ginger, chocolate, lime.
Girls, your type – small, dark, inclined to pout.
Sydney, last year – your favourite place and time.
Spring is your season. For some reason, you love sneezing.
Windchimes freak you out.
And I love you for all those reasons, but I doubt
I could make them the poem about you.

But I might write a haiku
completely about
how the back of your head looks
while you are asleep.
And I might write some deep, mythical Song of Solomon as long as
    Revelations
about the sheer elation of waking up and finding you between my sheets.
And I might knock out and shout a dirty limerick or two
about the joys above, and the joys beneath,

And if I really got on it, I could write you a sonnet
about how your butt shakes when you brush your teeth.

I could write all this and more.
And I could put the heat on for a bath for you
an hour before you step in the door,
and laugh at the things that make you laugh
that would usually only make me laugh if I was four,
and listen in the mornings to your dreams and nightmares talk,
fall in step with your walk,
start a love that would surely be
anybody's best piece of poetry
and see it through.
But I promise, I swear,
I'll work hard and take care
to never write the poem
about you.

2

NO ANGELS

Wrestling the Angel

In every woman's house there lives an angel.
They hear her white robes whisper on their stairs.
She smothers life and lust in clouds of household dust
and chokes impassioned songs with rationed prayers.
In every woman's throat her wings are beating.
There's really just one thing a girl can do.
Take your heart and shield it.
Grab a sword and wield it.
Get her before she gets you.

Please hold my handbag, I'm wrestling the angel
that's nesting like a hen in the corner of my life.
She bends to me and simpers – *will you never change, girl?*
You can't change this strange world. Why not be a wife?
She holds my arms and says they're never made to wrestle,
I should curl and nestle, quiet as a mouse,
be a vestal virgin, be an empty vessel,
be the heart and hearth of every daddy's house.

She gets between my pen and hungry pages.
She tells me, *leave the big themes to the men –*
that birds who learn to sing in sugar cages
should never need to spread their wings again.
In every woman's mouth her words are bitter,
they burn and blister like a new tattoo.
I hear her say, *stay pure,*
the others matter more.
Get her before she gets you.

Please hold my hair back, I'm wrestling the angel
who'd rather settle this without a speck of blood,
but yet she'd have our hearts out, pluck our juicy parts out,
damn us in our flesh like damming up a flood.
Some of us are born girls, some of us remain girls,
I'll never start to grow if she doesn't let me go.
She lectures me on cleanness, shows me how to dream less,
says no when I mean yes, and yes when I mean no.
And every baby girl's born with an angel.
Her shadow trails through all a child might do.
She'll find you, she'll blind you,
she'll gag you and she'll bind you –
but others won before you, others run behind you,
and they'll hold you up while you wrestle with your angel.
Do it, whatever you do.
Once you watch her going,
your wings might start growing.
Get her before she gets you.

Knives

It started at the circus, her attraction.
Not to the woman on her back, upright,
tied to a moving target, but the knives
around her, like a carousel of light,
edges and air whirling like wheeling birds.
Mouth sweet and sticky, pupils drunk with night,
she whispered five new words.
I want to throw knives.

She was five. She strived to grow,
learnt to thrive, took the best cutlery to throw,
scarred the floor. They couldn't hold her down.
The air that fogged the windows seemed to lift her.
She moved as swift as sound.
I want to be a shapeshifter, she thought.
Do backflips. Shuck my skin off like a sheath,
lay bare the light beneath. Just not be what
I'm meant to be. Be anything but me.

Fifteen. Winged muscle, skin like fitted chrome.
Leaving her home, ready to have some fun,
she stretched her sharpness in the morning sun
and shot out of the door, a darting arrow,
an empty shell, the bullet and the gun.

She flew. Everything seemed graced, replaced, new,
but there was no sticking place to screw her courage to.
Later they found her outside British Home Stores
catching and throwing air, her white face snared
In a dead stare. They took her in,
not sure what they could do. What she could do.

They touched her thinness, shuddered at her chill.
If she'd gone this far, maybe she could kill,
or pills might kill the things that she'd been through.
They held her with the thieves and broken wives,
and, writing reams about her mind's unfitness,
they gave her poster paints and plastic knives.

A girl had seen her run that day – a witness
who'd longed for grace, and glimpsed her face within
those shining planes, and gasped to see it there,
feeling the metal singing in her skin,
making her sharp where once she'd been a drifter.
I want to be a shapeshifter,
she thought. *Do backflips. Shuck my skin off like a sheath,*
lay bare the light beneath. Just not be what
I'm meant to be. Be anything but me.

Red Dress Blues

Last night I put on my red dress, strode through the bebop of blaring cars,
high heels clipping through clutter, dressed for the gutter, drinking
    the stars,
ready to taste the bad girls' breath and slam my shot glass down,
lose the day in the night's dense depths, and let tomorrow drown.

Today I've got bed-head like a nightshade vine.
I stink of bonfire smoke and rotgut wine,
but my mental choir is singing, *Damn, I'm fine.*
You've got to have front to wear a dress like mine.
I don't give a damn what the teacher said,
life is short and we're a long time dead.
I'm no angel, but I'm free to tread.
My dress has to be red.

And now I'm crumpled and bleeding from my battered satin feet,
sugar coating my split-skinned lips like mica gilding the street,
coffee in hand, heart in my throat, cushiony beat so loud
it blares right through the greyness like silk in a suit-clad crowd.

It's one fist clapping, not a Valentine.
You don't need trappings like a concubine
or bags and wrappings boasting rich design,
but you've got to have guts to wear a dress like mine.
I don't give a damn what the preacher said,
I'm reeling from a night in a stranger's bed,
that face above me like a figurehead.
My dress has to be red.

Today I woke in my red dress, flew past a milk-float into the sun,
numbers scrunched in my pocket, into the office, morning begun.
I'm getting the strangest glances from the other girls in pastels
but my head is full of dancers and the air is piled with castles.

I shook it from my toes to my rolling spine.
I acted devilish and felt divine.
You've got to make sweat to let your hot skin shine.
You've got to have hips to wear a dress like mine.
I don't give a damn what Nietzsche said,
there is a goddess and she's not dead.
Give me roses – screw your bread.
My dress has to be red.

Cherries in the Snow

The bus driver pulls off too fast. She falls,
grabbing the walls – she's far too old to stand.
Someone gives up their seat. In grubby shawls,
she lurches in, and with a knotted hand
dives for a compact carbuncled with pearls,
and lipstick – Cherries in the Snow, her brand
since she was just a mousy, breastless girl
craving the sleek red wax, the golden band
belting its lacquered black, its lazy twirl
or scarlet silk. And, later, the surprise
of men in bars. A pout, a slick flicked curl,
a red flag whipped before their startled eyes
and they were hers. She lets herself remember
the one who truly left and can't come back
but stirs in her with every dank November,
with poppies, small explosions on the black
of winter coats. Bathed in reflected light,
she smiles, her mouth a medal's scarlet plaque,
the old wars over, but her paint still bright.

No Dress Code

Something's got to give and it's the dress code.
I'm strong enough to live without the dress code.
'Cause I'm sick of calling my therapist
every time I want to have sex,
or hammering out a relationship
with my ex's girlfriend's girlfriend's ex,
and I'm sick of being told I must like boys
by girls in flannel shirts and bomber jackets
and being lectured on self-expression
by those who look like rows of Cornflakes packets,
and I'm sick of boys who stroke their chins
and say *Interesting. Ever considered...*
saying the same old lines,
each word freighted with revelation
like I'm hearing it for the first time.

Well.

If clothes make the woman,
then let me be unmade.
Make me sleazy as stained silk,
limp as dropped linen,
unknot the clots of my braid,
set my hair free,
unzip, unclasp, unravel me.

When I ask you for instruction
I'm begging for damnation,
but life without destruction
is just an imitation,
so let me put my face into your hands

and plant this one questioning kiss on your brow.
Time was, I'd have thrown your sword in the dirt,
strode off alone, high-heeled and unhurt,
a porcelain-faced corset-laced female impersonator
everything tight, holding me right like the loving asphyxiator
of hardcore porn. No more. I've been reborn
as the unrepentant detonator
of the bomb you buried and forgot till now.

Will you accept
no dress code?
No mess, no
stress, no
fuss, and my nasty habit of never, ever saying
Excuse me, but –
keeping my mouth shut,
letting my heart pound on.
Will you, and will you be proud?
I haven't waited a lifetime
to be allowed,
but if time's what you need,
I'm willing to concede an hour or two
'cause I don't want to be somewhere
where I can't look at you.

Someone told me this, so it's gotta be true,
that it all comes down to this last taboo –
what knot of flesh you've got, and what you do
with it. That's it. It's that complex.
Whoever we've been, whoever we'll be,
forget it. It's all about sex.

Well, I think about it all the time, but sex – no,
my soul it's not, my soul has got
no dress code.
I feel like me, not cock or cunt
not braced bloke's back or lipsticked front
and no hard facts to bear the brunt
of how or why I'm here.
So be with me and please, don't fear
this sorry absence of certainty,
'cause it's not even about being queer,
or looking for more easy-to-swallow knowledge,
it's not about Church or State or your mates or Fate
or whatever poststructuralist new-historicist
gender theory stuff you learnt in college.

We can ignore that till the crack of doom.
If you just put those labels we needed away,
I can hug you to me like a coat all day,
and in return I'll make my life the room
where you can walk around naked.

The Fat Lady's Song

One ordinary day she woke up tearless,
done with the kitchen scales, the chafing shame,
the stares – *they should just pay!* – so, acting fearless,
she slapped a smile on, chose a bigger name,

A name for striped marquees and circus patter
and slicked-back sideshow barker's ballyhoo –
*Come in and see Big Belle! There's no one fatter
From here to Timbuctoo! Sir – how 'bout you?*

Flesh brimming through her baby-doll short sheath,
oil sheened her folds of flab like rare pink pearl.
She worked the crowd, protected by a wreath
of smoke and awe, a pouting party girl

lumbering like an unleashed dancing bear.
The stories that they spread of her were wild –
midgets, giants, strongmen everywhere.
There's a whole lot of me to love, she smiled.

Later, she married an Italian cook
with floury hands, who loved to watch her eat,
almost as big as her. He lived to look,
and bake her pastries. Said he'd keep her sweet.

They reinforced their floors, stayed in at nights,
reshaped a stunted world to give them space.
She hummed and sang the tunes of circus sites,
swathed in a robe, rejoicing in her place.
Sometimes she missed the lions under lights,
their hungry eyes. Her sure, surprising grace.

Mad

When I was five years old my mother taught me how to scream.
I was strangled by my anger, I was mangled in hot steam,
I was a writhing little horror with flailing feet and fists
'cause the sky seemed like a mirror that my breath just couldn't mist,
so I couldn't write my poems with my finger on the world –
and all because some kid had said to me, *You're just a girl.*

When I was five years old I learnt a skill all girls should own,
to feel that shrill determined drill break complacent bone,
like when you pray that she'll stop talking just so you can throw the phone,
or you say it while you're walking, 'cause you never walk alone.
You never walk alone. You never – ever – ever walk alone.

So this is for the women who've been walking after dark
when your steps get louder, your breath draws in,
the keys in your hand print a brand on your skin –
but all they want to do is come up behind you,
all they want to do is come in around you,
and if you're lucky, they go.
And then one of them always shouts down the street,
like he's the one who knows,
Ah, I'm sorry for my friends, mate. Sorry for my friends.
Well, baby, I'm sorry for my friends too.
Because they say they're mad.
They come up to me and they say they're mad
and I think – *my God, I'm much more mad than you.*
But it's true.
They're mad because they're hungry and they'll never eat their fill,
They're mad because they're angry and they're told to take a pill.
They're mad because he won't come home, they're mad because he will,
They're mad because they're screaming, but inside where it can kill.

So this is for the women who've been squinting in the sun,
who've been scrubbing out their linen like they're nine months gone,
and their walls are tight, the lock needs picking,
but they'd be all right if that clock stopped ticking.
This is for the ones who want a moment's reprieve
that won't let them forget how it felt to believe
in what they were told when the world made sense,
before the words got so dark and dense
they could only breathe and live and grieve
and love and leave in the present tense.
This is for the women behind the door
who know that peace is a one-side war,
and who build their homes out of sticks and straw
and pray the rain won't get through.
And who say they're mad,
who lower their heads and they say they're mad.
Oh, baby.
Everybody's mad like you.

And if you look for a lack for your love, or a rock to anchor your anger to,
if you want it all, or just want him to call – and perhaps bring a
        takeout too –
if you think that the walls will collapse if you cry,
and want nothing but bathtubs and books and blue sky,
if you buy fresh herbs in terracotta pots at Tesco's for £2.99 a pop
        and take them home and put them on the kitchen windowsill
        and watch them die –
then this one's all about you.

I said when I was five years old my mother taught me how to scream,
to find the art that's in your heart by ripping out the seam
that they sewed to keep you quiet, sewed to keep you low,
to shut the root of the cord they cut when they thought you
    wouldn't know,
and you're mad because you're feeling battered black and blue
'cause you shattered that glass ceiling but the cracks won't let you through,
and you're mad about them knowing, or they've just not got a clue.
You're mad because you're owing, but you don't know what you're due.
You're mad because they don't come home, you're mad because they do.
And you say you're mad.
You open your mouth and you say you're mad.

Oh, baby.
I'd be much more mad than you.

Wilderness Years

No, Granny, no maybes, I'm not getting married,
or toeing the family line.
My cousins have babies, they're fretting and harried,
and have bigger stretchmarks than mine.
If I ever take on all I've learnt to reject,
then I'd do it for money, or fame,
or a shedload of sex, and a skip full of cheques,
but not for some loser's last name.
While they're betting on house prices falling,
I'm sweating in second-hand furs,
thinking, am I remiss? Or perhaps I'm just stalling –
with all I dismiss, am I missing my calling?
I used to be focused, neurotic and driven,
now I can't say no to a damn thing I'm given.
And what will I do with my life? Well, I'm living.
I'm loving the wilderness years.

Yes, Granny, the skirt I've got on is from Primark.
The coat that I wear – it ain't mink.
Yes, I should have deciphered that Don't Tumble Dry mark
and not cut my hair in the sink.
I'm just a bit ravaged, a little dishevelled,
I revel in all things offensive.
My hangover's savage, my work's entry-level,
my tastes are debased – yet expensive.
When I know that a night on the dancefloor's in store
my inner Miss Whiplash just purrs,
though I know I'll get ratted and battered and sore
with my hands and knees knackered from hitting the floor
and I'll drink and dial people I ought to ignore
and I'll wake up and vow not to drink any more

'cause I know I'll feel crap until Tuesday at four,
but hey – them's the wilderness years.

I like to dress up in tight dresses and leathers
for dyke bars and crappy old flicks.
I like to go out to burlesques in white feathers
and twirl the girls' tassels for kicks.
I like lefties and bohos and hippies and hobos
who share my artistic delusions,
and emos and screamers and dreamers and homos
who've learnt to embrace life's confusions,
'cause I like when the darkness might blind me.
I like when the boundary blurs.
I like leaving duty and conscience behind me,
If I don't keep moving that nonsense might find me.
I like when this world in its hugeness astounds me,
amuses me, bruises me, screws and confounds me.
I smile as its brutal great beauty surrounds me.
I'm free in these wilderness years.

I tend to start bluffing at City Boy parties
when some Tarquin asks what I make.
I make something from nothing and that's where my heart is –
they ask like my whole world's at stake.
My friends work for Goldman's, they swot for the bar,
I like things a tad more diverse.
You could be a contender, a bender, a star,
so why just surrender to things as they are?
When I see a young girl I just want to warn her
to not watch the dance from the wallflower's corner.
You don't want to end up a middle-aged mourner
who never had wilderness years.

So Granny, you've got my CD, you've heard some rhymes
that aren't sacrilegious or blue.
And I like how you ask me how she's doing sometimes.
I know what it costs you. I do.
But our life is our baby, our work. It's organic.
We both like to shout in the rain –
Please Granny, don't panic, I'm just a bit manic,
I don't really want to be sane!
And when I'm too old and too poor to rebel
I'll just take that as it occurs,
When nobody's looking I'll still unleash hell,
I'll be having my hash cake and toking as well –
but I'll grow old with grace and won't dye my greys black
and I'll live in the moment, but yeah, I'll look back,
and I'll tell you one thing, Granny – I will not regret jack,
when I think of my wilderness years.

Angels and Men

If I speak
with the tongues of angels and men, that's all very well.
But I'm not either – so why the talk of hell
and the lie you tell me
that nobody can hurt me if I stay behind this wall?
You say, 'Keep still, and the rain won't come.
Sit and be silent or the sky might fall...'
I should stay in my box, tucked away with your locks,
and keep my ears cocked for my wake-up call.
'Cause if I can't say anything nice,
then I shouldn't say anything at all.

But I tell you that I do pray.
And when I raise my voice then the thing you call my choice
just rolls away.
How can I play dumb, when heaven lies around me?
If I speak
with the tongues of angels and men, and I have not love,
then you'd say 'Amen,' and I'd just stay numb.
I'd play a sounding drum at the heart of an orchestra that drowned me.

And I know the secrets at your start,
the tools that made your life an art,
but if maybe you want to see
what pulls my soul apart,
it's when she stands in front of me
and holds my face and looks at me
and says, 'Oh girl, you break my heart.
Oh, girl, you break my heart.'

Your love quotes saints and kings
and all the things that my love's ducked.
My love pulls your love's wings
and makes him eat the fruit she's plucked.
Your love writes sermons. My love sings.
We stand and watch them do their things
and that's all very well,
'cause I've gotta tell you
without love
we're fucked.

So I'd rather mince down main streets
and shout 'I'm here, I'm queer,'
go out for milk and bread
with my pants on my head
and a red brassiere
and paint this town bright pink
when I think it's the only thing that'll keep me here
than not have love.
When you don't have love
then you just do what you've got to.
So I see my love's got enough to eat
and I kiss my love in the crowded street
and I sit my love in the window seat
'cause life's just too short not to.

You want to see a prophecy
in which I might believe?
It's when she stands in front of me
and looks a little while at me
and smiles that special smile at me
and tells me I'm her Eve.
She tells me I'm her Eve.

I've said it before and I'll say it again –
If I speak with the tongues of angels and men
then that's all very well.
But without love my voice is weak
and I clunk and creak like a rusted bell.
I can preach about joy and sorrow,
I can teach about life and death,
but if I speak without love,
if I live without love,
then my words are a waste of breath.
I'd just get bored of my own discord
and leave this world still seething –
'cause if you can't say anything nice
then why don't you just stop breathing?

I won't keep still
'cause the rain will come.
I won't run for shelter
for that sky will fall.
Then I'll pelt helter-skelter into the sun
and make the ground rock with my wakeup call.
But if I let the world win, break my soul and spin me round and
    force me underground and win me over to know a love that's
    not within me,
If I did that, and still had an ounce of sense left in me
Then I wouldn't fucking speak
at all.

3

ORDINARY JOYS

Unless There's Dancing

I danced everywhere as a kid,
when my ego meant less than my id.
I'd skip, jump and hop
till my folks wished I'd stop,
but both of them bawled when I did,
when puberty came with its onslaught of shame
as dreary as Methodist hymns,
about what I should say, and if I was gay,
and what I should do with my limbs.
But I thought,
I'm not growing unless there's dancing,
I'm not going, no way.
So I'm going to get old, but still I'm not sold,
I just want to go out and play.
I'm told when I'm grown I'll have things of my own,
like long nights and a home and romance –
I just want to be free; it's all adult to me.
I'm not growing up if I can't dance.

Gay Rage was my teenage agenda,
my mates talking race, class and gender.
We'd get in frantic states
and semantic debates
when some poof called some gaylord a bender.
I was only eighteen, and my dreams were unclean,
but my jeans stayed pristine every night.
We spent long left-wing hours in our ivory towers
being deliciously right.
But I said,
I'm not marching unless there's dancing.
I'm quite happy inside.

If I get to shout 'Charge,' and start a *ménage,*
you bet I'll be going to Pride.
I hate to demur, Miss Chairperson Sir,
could we just jump about in our pants?
I don't mean to insult ya,
it's *well* counter-culture –
I'm not marching if I can't dance.

These days I'm a Saturday hippy –
I'm the right mix of bolshy and dippy.
I can stand in a line, waving a sign,
then slope off somewhere and get trippy.
And when we're done yanking the grassroots of life
then we go and strip off by the lake,
risking nailing in jail with our micro-brewed ale
and our mouthfuls of magical cake,
'cause I said,
I'm not fighting unless there's dancing.
I'll be writhing in tents.
I'll be over the limit, over the hill,
and over the festival fence.
I've never been tested by being arrested,
it may screw my self-possessed stance –
the gate staff can stick it,
check out my Crew ticket,
I'm not fighting if I can't dance.

Now I live with the working girl blues,
I pay money for stuff I don't use.
You can scrape off your tax,
get the sweat off my back,
but you can't take my shiny red shoes.
And I'll go on this way till I drop down one day
and I get one last chance to repent.

When I get to my feet, then I'll say to St. Pete
in that frankly unlikely event –
I'm not coming unless there's dancing,
Think I'll chance it below.
Yeah, I know that your guest list is one of the best
but there's nobody on it I know.
And I hear that you're mean on the old tambourine
but if everyone has to behave,
Then I'm going to choose fires over heavenly choirs,
'cause the devil does do a good rave.

I'm not dying unless there's dancing.
I'm not living if there's no beat,
no trusting the air to hold you up there,
no landing unscathed on your feet.
So life isn't easy but disco's still cheesy
and hip-hop's a breeze and punk rock's still sleazy.
I only need one kind of dancing to please me –
not blues, ballet, techno or trance,
but that crazy wild style that I learnt as a child
and saved for myself in advance.
So I'm prancing around with my brain drowned in sound
entrusting my balance to chance.
You know it's not dumb while my heart is still drumming.
I'm not coming if I can't dance.

The Origin of the World

All day she lies in front of strangers' eyes,
headless and nameless, spread apart like wings
to show her not-so-private opening,
made art when one man laid her on this throne
and opened her like a reluctant heart,
down to the darkness bridged beneath the bone
where everything we've ever known must start.

There's a man standing next to me.
An ordinary man.
And feeling kind of wicked, I want to turn and say:

Hey. Mister. Get this.
When you look into the abyss,
the abyss also looks into you.
And to be blunt,
you came out of a place like this too.
It opened like a fist to wave you through,
splitting the lock of after and before
its pushing pulse became the beat that bore your lifetime's ticking clock.
They held you up, too hard, too fast, too high –
you saw the sky, too far away and bright.
Just listen to that first indignant cry –
limbs flailing, mouth wailing,
your whole self railing in that blinding light.

You forgot this mess, this bliss, Mister Man.
You've been seeking whatever's not this wherever you can.
But see what you miss in the quest for that
fleshless, tasteless, glistening fist
displayed in porn and Playboy plastic-wrap.

This gift was your first geographic shift,
now it's a foreign country you can't map.
And if it had been up to me,
I'd have called it something like *anemone*
Or *imbroglio*. Wrap your tongue round that.
You and the men before you called it *twat*. The hole.
The courtly arbour, the safe harbour in every port, the sport, the goal,
The long dark midnight of your tortured soul.
Your doctor's fingers and your scholar's fear.
You stand like Dante at the mouth of Hell –
Abandon Hope, All Ye Who Enter Here.

There's a man standing next to me.
An ordinary man.
And feeling kind of warm, I want to turn to him and say:

Don't look. Drink.
Think textures – velvet, petals, satin, ink,
metal melting to lakes on the lip.
Smell incense like the inside of a church,
sense the earth's lurch, its microscopic tip.
Speak in its private tongue of clicks and pops,
glottal stops on the mouth's ridged ceiling.
As for the feeling,
think moist mornings with the moon still in the sky,
the ripples carved in time by a beating butterfly.
Think of a red open throat singing.

Now the light's thinning as the day grows older.
There's not much time at all. So Mister, please.
Stand shoulder to shoulder with me in front of this wall.
Stare into the eye of your beginning
and fall on your knees.

Hair

I leave my hair
everywhere.
Take care if you take me home,
because I can take you unaware
long after you think I've gone.
With pillowbook calligraphy
woven through white mesh.
Like the midnight ink of a drunk tattoo
I can bloom under your flesh
till you breathe weeds, not air
that coat your throat and make you choke if you swear
you never met the owner of this hair.
I am a minimalist's worst nightmare.

I got this hair
everywhere.
A town without a name.
This hair dragged caravans, snagged reins, tossed
and kicked like a Camorra killer,
fell like a Catholic girl's mantilla.
This hair is thick with lives
that history lost.
But exotica comes with a cost,
because every little girl wants to be precious and rare
not *interesting*, or *deep*,
and God knows, not with Brillo-pad hair
and someone else's hips and boobs sprouting in your sleep and don't
    even *talk* about
Down There.

Other girls got to be Barbie.
Other girls were The Girl Next Door.
I was the Other Woman shortly after Primary Four.
So beware if your sheets are white
and this barnet hasn't been there yet.
You want to practise safe sex with me tonight?
Stop by your local all-night chemist's and buy me a hairnet.

But if I get deep in your marrow
and there's more you need to know
I don't leave tea-leaves, or tarot,
or breadcrumbs in the snow.
No, you can find me by my hair.
Be brave. Follow me, and I'll be
Rapunzel. Salome. Scheherazade. Yours. There.
For weeks, months, years, you'll unknit the tapestry
of one night with me. Prepare.
I leave my hair
everywhere.
So there.

One Song

She stands. She blinks.
She thinks, *this spotlight's bright.*
She shows she won't ask much of us tonight.
She's 'only going to sing one song'. All right.
Pub karaoke has no Ladies' Night.

The men go on.
It's just the way they do.
It's never just one song, it's always two
or three. For them, it's only taking part.
They don't apologise before they start.

She owns her song.
She hones it like a queen,
a sleazy star of some speakeasy scene,
a brothel-house of mocking-birds. A diva,
a belting, brazen, unashamed believer.

It hurts, her song.
It chains us every day,
and yet she wears that chain like Cartier.
It's what we've done and what we've failed to do,
the hearts we nurse and hide, the colour blue.

We could belong.
We think we might be strong,
our whoops and whistles swooping through the throng.
Clapped hands slap everyone who's done us wrong.
That rising of applause. Her smile. One song.

Things I'm Not Afraid Of

There are things I'm not afraid of.
That's not an idle boast.
If I showed what I was made of
then my heart's more faint than most,
but still my hands are writing, atoms writhing, cells dividing,
words jazzing and jiving around my head
as I write letters like gestures to the dead,
like thank-you notes for thriving.
Well, I'm solvent, just about,
paying rent, going out,
father and mother alive –
I mean, that's what it's all about,
surviving.

There are things I'm not afraid of.
Like milk. And kittens.
And five-hundred-piece jigsaws of hills.
And I've just about got to the stage
where I can watch kids' TV without pills.
I'm not scared of Officer Krupke,
the Keystone Kops or PC Plod,
teenage shitkickers, C of E Vicars,
Virginia Woolf, Tobias Wolff,
the whole cast of *EastEnders*
or the Old Testament God.

I do, however, still have a couple of problems with:
Death.
Morning breath. The morning after.
Inappropriate laughter.
Doctors.

The *Daily Mail* and everyone who reads it
(except my granny,
who just likes the crosswords).
Waking up and confronting my own mortality.
Giving in too young and too numbly to senseless practicality.
VD.
Certain regimes of dictatorial principalities
and reality TV.
Losing my keys, my job, my marbles and my health,
losing that which separates me from another.
Turning into my mother.
Turning into anyone else.

There are things we're all afraid of.
You can think you're all right,
then you wake up, and you're up against the night,
and you can scream, you can cry, you can say
you never asked for this,
that you wanted settled nights and muted lights
and loving arms to hold you,
not friendless four a.m. psychosis.
But just hold the moment,
like light you can't break,
like skin you can't split,
like all you can't keep,
because today could be it.
Or, it could not,
but either way,
who wants to sleep?

Drink deep.
Rise and shine. Stand tall.
Show the scars you sustained
when you slipped in the rain

when you were looking at the stars,
and barely even felt yourself fall.
Don't rationalise.
Open your eyes, mouth, thighs,
and say *yes, yes, yes*
to it all.

To screaming as you dive when you choose to lose the ledges.
To running like you're five and the playground's lost its edges.
To all the things that make you want to hug yourself
and roll on the rug and bellow like a baby in a church
to make the ground lurch and the sky shake.
To that, and cake.

There are things I'm not afraid of
because Sacco and Cato and Sappho and Plato
read them for me,
because Harvey Milk and Carol Shields and Oscar Wilde
said them for me,
because Salvador Dali and Frida Kahlo
spread them in gold and red and bled them for me
and how can I give in to tears, how can I give in to fears
when they shed them for me?
I can't.

And in conclusion
there are things I'm not afraid of
because cats aren't.

Mind the Gaps

All of the posters seem to reprimand.
We seem so harmless, dumb and doped with dreams.
We're watching you. Please mind your bags. Please stand.
Orwell would choke on this. But still it seems
to suit us, when we fail to recognise
the other humans sweating in this trap –
the simple fact of meeting someone's eyes
perversion, weakness, asking for a slap.
And yet sometimes there's still a sweet surprise,
like when the begging busker gets a clap
acknowledging his shared humanity,
or when an old one's entrance prompts a rise,
or deadpan drivers drawl, *Please mind the gap
between the train times and reality.*

It suits me well, this hourless, lightless city,
this place where no one wants to know your name,
where nothing's under pressure to be pretty
and bad behaviour rarely equals shame,
where people shuffle in like shocked survivors,
eyes raised in panic for the right direction,
where schoolgirls swear like New York taxi drivers
and drag queens bask in militant perfection
and boys spray paint and bullets of saliva.
Each coloured path maps out a new direction,
their pulses mark my ticking metronome.
Preparing for the surface like a diver,
I slowly rise. I like the intersection
between things, where I'm always most at home.

Buying Tomatoes

I'm buying these tomatoes for the kids who aren't my kids yet,
who haven't met my eyes, or waved a hand inside my belly,
who haven't breathed the air I breathe walking to the deli,
who haven't learnt the things I've earned
or heard the things I did yet.
I'm picking these tomatoes for the kids who run around the tombs
by the old house in Italy as I once did, in Sunday best.
I'm picking these tomatoes for the kids who haven't met me yet,
the kids who never let me rest,
who wait for me in other rooms.
I want to get enough to give my small conquistadors,
their hands black with digging to the earth's core.

Let your past hold you fast when you feel the world turn.
When the earth gives you birth, to the earth you return.
It's a long way to come, it's a long way to go –
you wanna be a Madonna, it's a hard row to hoe.
But I'm buying these tomatoes for the kids who aren't my kids yet –
the circle of lamplight I've not learnt to guard,
the truths and the ties that have yet to hold hard,
the hope of the lives I might grow.

I'm cooking these tomatoes for a lover I've not met yet
who stands in the kitchen, watching my hands,
kissing my neck where the sweet sweat lies.
The drop in the motion that time understands
as I put down the knife and I close my eyes.
The lemon and salt in the arch of the wrist.
The veins intact with their stacked red ore.
The teeth in my jaw turned to pearls with a kiss.
The kick of life at the pulse's core.

The hours drift past like breath on glass
as the shadows stretch and the night pulls in
and sifts through linen where blessings pass,
filling the windows etched in our skin.

In the raw heat of hunger, you let your hands burn.
In the sheets you first stained, you remain and return.
It's a long way to come, it's a long way to go.
Blow your cover for your lover – that's a hard row to hoe.
But I'm cooking these tomatoes for a lover I've not met yet,
for time still unmeasured, a world still untamed,
the part of my heart that's never ashamed,
the hope that I'll stop saying no.

I'm eating these tomatoes for the woman who I'm not yet,
who makes the right decisions, and whose white sheets last a week.
I'm filling up a glass to toast the things I haven't got yet,
I've got a plate of certainty, and there's no need to speak.
I'm a lone star of stalk, I'm half a wishbone,
I'm cooking these tomatoes and I'll eat them on my own
but I talk to the night in a still-lipped prayer
just to live in my body like a kitchen chair,
to live with shadows – mute, unnamed,
to live with silence but not with shame.
If I let the wine stain, then it's nobody's fault –
If I'm crying, it's the onions,
and God knows a sauce needs salt.

Patience and pain take a long life to learn.
From the dark we arise, to the dark we return.
It's a long way to come, it's a long way to go,
when you're craving for a haven it's a hard row to hoe,
but I'm miming the lives of the lovers and mothers

'cause I want to have one thing to give to the others
and this is the one truth I know.

I'll be buying tomatoes as long as I'm able
so do me the honour and sit at my table.
Leave the hours in the street.
Take the weight off your feet.
Hey. Where are you from?
Come in and eat.

Not Yet

My father's voice is weak. *The car's a wreck.*
We could have lost your mother. But she's fine.
I've seen my lover stretchered, head and neck
in plastic stocks, and everything of mine
felt lost. I've known that sense of impotence
(my hands stretched, couldn't touch her) the regret
that somehow we're not there for accidents –
the phone turned off, the hunch we fail to get
that something's wrong, the end of self-defence:
Give me the strength to love them, but not yet.

You know that damage is already done
when somebody you love scrapes clear of death.
Just one inch more… you see how everyone
walks on a tightrope slender as a breath,
and ours have just been shaken, mine and his,
with this quick glimpse – no mother now, no wife.
A rigged quiz, this, the same old shameless swizz
each time. This time, a rubber-bladed knife.
You see, he says, *how fragile it all is,*
this house of cards, this mockery, this life.

This was the year my parents aged the most.
They speak of knee replacements, walking dogs,
investing in a cottage on the coast –
You'll get the money when we pop our clogs.
I squirm and beg them not to talk like that,
resent them both for teaching me the things
that made me human – not an alley cat
that comes and goes. I'm still a child that clings

to lives like bunched balloons, a pigtailed brat
who bellows when her fingers drop the strings.

I wonder how they live, the people left.
I know too well I've never lost someone
I've loved enough to render me bereft.
Why aren't they screaming? How do they go on?
And yet they do – you see it every day,
a miracle we're eager to forget.
I'm not convinced that I could go that way,
but no one pays their way out of this debt.
I do what all lost causes do, and pray.
Give me the strength to lose them. But not yet.

Some Nights the Stars Are Here

In the evenings they hang like gauze
past the balconies and rooftop doors,
friends ahead of us, my arm in yours,
spitting street-stalls forming soft applause,
like our happiness deserves a cheer.
Some nights the stars are here.

Nights at festivals bleed through to days,
strobe-lights wheeling in the smoke-filled haze.
In the hills the eyes of firelights blaze,
cold ground throbbing in the bassline praise.
The dark's colossal, but it's never sheer.
Some nights the stars are here.

Sometimes nightmares leave us choked and bowed.
Pain can wake us, make us cry out loud,
twist our sheets into a winding shroud,
morning waiting in a weight of cloud.
In your arms I turn my back on fear.
Some nights the stars are here.

The pasts we're hiding and the tunes we play,
the scars inside us help us map the way
to lead us through the dark. The worn, the stray,
the bruised, the hurt, the lost – we'll see the day,
I promise. Even when they're not quite clear,
Some nights the stars are here.

Notes

Don't Tell Me the Truth about Love: A reworking of W.H. Auden with excerpts from 'Love Don't Cost A Thing', 'Nature Boy', 'Love is All Around', and 'All You Need is Love.'

Goodnight Moon: Title from the 1947 bedtime story book *Goodnight Moon* by Margaret Wise Brown.

Wrestling the Angel: Based on Virginia Woolf's essay about being a woman writer, 'Killing the Angel in the House'. 'I did my best to kill her. My excuse, were I to be had up in a court of law, would be that I acted in self-defence. Had I not killed her she would have killed me.'

Red Dress Blues: Inspired by Kim Addonizio's poem, 'What Women Want'.

Angels and Men: 'If I speak in the tongues of men and angels, but have not love, I have become sounding brass or a tinkling cymbal.' 1 Corinthians.

The Origin of the World: Based on the painting *L'Origine du Monde* by Gustave Courbet, 1866.

Born Again: Includes a line from Louis MacNeice's 'Prayer before Birth'.